"Humor abounds in Hnath's creative sequel . . . His script is an irreverent yet respectful take on the source material . . . A worthy companion piece to the original, *A Doll's House, Part 2* is an imaginative postscript to a well-loved standard."

—**Maya Stanton,** *Entertainment Weekly*

"An incredibly enjoyable play . . . The true triumph of *A Doll's House, Part 2* is its refreshingly feminist political message."

—**Christian Lewis,** *Huffington Post*

THE CHRISTIANS

"Mr. Hnath is quickly emerging as one of the brightest new voices of his generation. What's fresh about his work is how it consistently combines formal invention with intellectual inquiry—both of which are often in short supply in contemporary American theatre."

—**Charles Isherwood,** *New York Times*

"*The Christians* is a white-knuckled drama about . . . a theological battle. But there are no clear winners or losers in Lucas Hnath's deeply affecting new play."

—**Elisabeth Vincentelli,** *New York Post*

"For all its control on the page, *The Christians* is about the uncontrollable, which is to say, how we imagine what life will look like once we enter the everlasting."

—**Hilton Als,** *The New Yorker*

"It's so rare to see religious beliefs depicted onstage without condescension that Lucas Hnath's new play becomes all the more intriguing."

—**Frank Scheck,** *The Hollywood Reporter*

"Lucas Hnath's soul-searching drama, *The Christians*, grabbed the eyeballs at the 2014 Humana Festival . . . the play's religious dialectic offers enough substance to satisfy true believers."

—**Marilyn Stasio,** *Variety*

RED SPEEDO

"A bright slip of a swimsuit seems a small garment on which to hang a knotty morality play, but the ingenious Lucas Hnath engineers this remarkable feat with *Red Speedo*, a taut, incisive drama."

—**Charles Isherwood,** *New York Times*

"Hnath's swift, slippery play moves in Mametian lunges of rapid dialogue and desperate gambits." **—Adam Feldman, *Time Out New York***

"*Red Speedo* is the latest addition to the increasingly substantial body of work by playwright Lucas Hnath. If you're serious about the theater, you have to see his shows and read his plays and look forward to whatever is next with anticipation. **—Michael Giltz, *The Huffington Post***

"As he did with *The Christians*, Hnath raises hugely important questions about our society and the occasionally perverse behavior it encourages."
—Zachary Stewart, TheatreMania.com

"Hnath lightly suggests—he's too subtle to use the big hammer—that the immoral imbalance of our current economy is stripping us down to our animal skins." **—Jesse Green, *Variety***

A PUBLIC READING OF AN UNPRODUCED SCREENPLAY ABOUT THE DEATH OF WALT DISNEY

"A blackly comic inversion of the public Disney persona, in the form of a stylized screenplay being read in an anonymous-looking corporate conference room . . . Walt would be doing cartoonish gyrations in his grave if he were to see how thoroughly Mr. Hnath (pronounced nayth) has subverted the popular image of Disney."
—Charles Isherwood, *New York Times*

"Minutes into the darkly humorous play it's clear that for the famous man who made Mickey Mouse, movies and the Magic Kingdom, everything was about him. Always. Especially during his last days on earth."
—Joe Dziemianowicz, *New York Daily News*

"A devastating portrait of a man for whom make-believe was more real than reality itself." **—Elisabeth Vincentelli, *New York Post***

"A blood-pumping and often hilarious evening of theater."
—Zachary Stewart, TheaterMania.com

"Enjoyably weird and hermetic . . . Nothing that ever came out of the Magic Kingdom was ever this animated."
—David Cote, *Time Out New York*

LUCAS HNATH received a 2017 Tony Award nomination for Best Play with *A Doll's House, Part 2*. Hnath's other plays include *Hillary and Clinton*, *The Thin Place*, *Red Speedo*, *The Christians*, *A Public Reading of an Unproduced Screenplay About the Death of Walt Disney*, *Isaac's Eye*, and *Death Tax*. He has been produced on Broadway at the John Golden Theatre and Off-Broadway at New York Theatre Workshop, Playwrights Horizons, Soho Rep, and Ensemble Studio Theatre. His plays have also been premiered at the Humana Festival of New Plays, Victory Gardens, and South Coast Repertory. He is a New York Theatre Workshop Usual Suspect, a member of Ensemble Studio Theatre, and an alumnus of New Dramatists. His awards include the Whiting Award, Guggenheim Fellowship, Kesselring Prize, Outer Critics Circle Award for Best New Play, Obie Award for Playwriting, Steinberg Playwright Award, and the Windham-Campbell Literary Prize.

A PUBLIC READING
OF AN UNPRODUCED
SCREENPLAY ABOUT
THE DEATH OF
WALT DISNEY

a play by **Lucas Hnath**

THE OVERLOOK PRESS
NEW YORK, NY

To Jyana Browne and Andrew Grusetskie

This edition first published in paperback in the United States in 2020 by
The Overlook Press, an imprint of ABRAMS
195 Broadway, 9th floor
New York, NY 10007
www.overlookpress.com

Abrams books are available at special discounts when purchased in quantity for premiums and promotions as well as fundraising or educational use. Special editions can also be created to specification. For details, contact specialsales@abramsbooks.com or the address above.

Cataloging-in-Publication Data is available from the Library of Congress

Book design and type formatting by Bernard Schleifer
Manufactured in the United States of America
ISBN 978-1-4683-1082-5
1 3 5 7 9 10 8 6 4 2

You can't just let nature run wild.
—WALT DISNEY

A PUBLIC READING
OF AN UNPRODUCED
SCREENPLAY ABOUT
THE DEATH OF
WALT DISNEY

A Public Reading of an Unproduced Screenplay About the Death of Walt Disney was presented by Soho Rep (Sarah Benson, Artistic Director; Cynthia Flowers, Executive Director; Caleb Hammons, Producer) in New York City, opening on May 10, 2013. It was directed by Sarah Benson; the set design was by Mimi Lien; the costume design was by Kaye Voyce; the lighting design was by Matt Frey; the sound design was by Matt Tierney; and the production stage manager was Heather Arnson. The cast was as follows:

WALT	Larry Pine
DAUGHTER	Amanda Quaid
RON	Brian Sgambati
ROY	Frank Wood

CHARACTERS

WALT, chain smokes the entire play.

ROY, brother, Band-aid over his left temple.

DAUGHTER, more like a parent than a child.

RON MILLER, son-in-law, dumb jock, a Golden Retriever of a person.

STAGE

Set up for a reading.
A table cluttered with the stuff a cast might need for
a day of table work. Chairs for the actors.

HOW TO PLAY IT

All actors present at the reading table for the entire duration of the
play. No one exits or enters.

Indented lines are screen directions read by Walt. Avoid pantomiming
or attempting to represent onstage those screen directions. Minimal
blocking is best; leave much to the imagination. The italicized stage
directions will tell you what actions should be enacted.

Read it swiftly without rushing. Let the lines flow seamlessly from one
to the next. Never let it get staccato.

Be especially careful of Walt's "cut to" lines. As a general rule, let
there be absolutely no air between the "cut to" and the lines that pre-
cede and follow it.

The script tells you where you can catch a breath (. . .); otherwise,
keep it moving.

Avoid trying to play "emotion" of the lines. Inflection takes time, and
you don't have that much time.

The rhythm and musical effect of the language is king.

Music. Repetitive. Piano. Strings. Lulling lullaby. Like a storm coming.
Trouble brewing. ACTOR/WALT *enters.*

WALT

Takes out a cigarette.
Lights cigarette.
Smokes.
*(*WALT *smokes.)*
Smokes.
(Adjusts volume of speakers as needed.)
(Down to business.)
(Readies his script.)

I'm Walt Disney.

This is a screenplay I wrote.
It's about me.

Fade in. Fade in on me,
Walt, fade in on Walt, fade in on Walt.
Walt. Close on Walt.

Walt is good.

Walt is doing good, looking good, looking good for his age,
age or no age looking good. Walt is
quick and smart and sharp and great.
And rich and loved
and richer than he's ever been
and more loved than he's ever been.
And he's doing great.
And he can have anything he wants.

Fade in on Walt, where, Walt
in a room, interior, day,
me in room, with Roy, the camera cuts to Walt's brother Roy, sitting
to his

left, Roy to left, in a room, interior, day or night, and night and day,
what room, doesn't matter what room, all kinds of rooms,
all sorts, and all sorts of times, and

cut music.

WALT
Scene 1, In which Walt decides to start
making Nature Documentaries.

ROY
awful late

WALT
Interior, night
working

ROY
middle of the night

WALT
thought you'd be asleep

ROY
having trouble

WALT
sleeping

ROY
just can't seem to

WALT
Interior, work office
Follow me Roy.

ROY
the dog, the

WALT
family

ROY
dog

WALT
Teddy

ROY
not doing well

WALT
the camera Cuts to a picture of Roy's dog Teddy

ROY
little back legs

WALT
Close on back legs

ROY

not working anymore, vet put it in a little wheel cart, little

WALT

yeah

ROY

pulls itself along with its front legs

WALT

can't let

ROY

having a real hard time, crying all night, stroke its ears, stroke its
legs til it sleeps

WALT

technology . . . can fix almost anything, anything, almost anything,
most, many things

ROY

still, scary

WALT

and Close on Walt and Close on Roy

ROY

doctors

WALT

saw one the other

ROY

you're

WALT

no just a

ROY

having

WALT

back problems, neck and shoulder,
doctor said it was some sort of calcification,
gave me pills,
taking pills,
pain pills, pills help,
a little, not much,
pills, a little drink, smoke, pills, pain

ROY

exercise

WALT
 oh sure
ROY
 That's good
WALT
 10 jumping jacks in the morning
ROY
 nice
WALT
 hot water baths
ROY
 nice
WALT
   Cut to
 And the wife says
ROY
 how is she?
WALT
 shouldn't work so much, she says
ROY
 haven't seen
WALT
 she travels
ROY
 okay
WALT
 visiting relatives
ROY
 nice, it must
WALT
 not really
ROY
 kinda lonely
WALT
 no
ROY
 just
WALT
   Cut to

And they all say,
well, he just does cartoons

ROY
they?

WALT
say

ROY
about

WALT
me

ROY
okay

WALT
it's like

ROY
they like

WALT
sure

ROY
everything you do is so

WALT
likeable

ROY
so wonderful about

WALT
but not so

ROY
it's good

WALT
important

ROY
makes money

WALT
really like to, need to, want to, should do

ROY
something different

WALT
a little, I guess, I would say, I'm thinking

ROY
more
WALT
expanding
ROY
where
WALT
into the real world.
ROY
. . .
WALT
. . .
ROY
. . . oh.
. . . *that.*
WALT
So far it's been
ROY
yeah
WALT
nothing but fairy tales and fairy things and
ROY
very likable
WALT
not interested in the political, politics, the political, that stuff, I
don't know, it's,
just not good, wouldn't, no, that type of thing, no
ROY
too, I'd say, risky
WALT
pushing your political views on others
ROY
it's
WALT
like sticking your finger up someone else's
ROY
talking about politics
WALT
just not important, in the end, I don't think, political stuff

ROY
sure
WALT
thinking about, real things, documentaries I guess, but not
ROY
right
WALT
but no, but maybe make a couple of movies about nature, travel,
animals,
going to places people would never go, where it's
too much trouble to go in real life
ROY
mountains
WALT
no one really wants to climb a mountain, 'cuz who has the time
ROY.
Alaska
WALT
sure, and
ROY
maybe other countries
WALT
eh . . .
ROY
you'd
WALT
rather we stay here, risky going
ROY
more expensive
WALT
not sure I care so much about
ROY
sure
WALT
don't need to leave America, people aren't so interested in
ROY
okay
WALT
    Cut to

and your kid

ROY

yeah?

WALT

maybe put your kid, your kid, just graduated from, what's it
called

ROY

Pomona College

WALT

sure, good thing for him to do, good place to start a

ROY

gosh, sure would appreciate

WALT

let him maybe, put his name on as producer of these here nature
documentaries
make it his little thing, maybe
our little thing, me and you and him and me and you,
our little family thing

ROY

nice

WALT

no women allowed

ROY

oh

WALT

ha ha ha ha ha

ROY

ha

WALT

ha ha

ROY

ha

WALT

ha ha and you

ROY

financing it

WALT

you worry about

ROY

I could

WALT

find people to show the

ROY

could be challenging, distribution

WALT

don't care, don't bother me with

ROY

'cuz people aren't interested in documentaries like they are cartoons

WALT

just slap my name on it and

ROY

sure, but

WALT

my name goes a long way, don't you

ROY

no, I know, it's

WALT

Cut to

ROY

and now we're

WALT

And we Cut to

one month later

ROY

and now we're filming

WALT

in Alaska

and filming one now in Yosemite,

and filming one now in New Mexico

and filming one now in

ROY

we're just making so many

WALT

films about bears and seals and bees and wolves

ROY

people enjoy seeing nature and animals and

WALT

shit

ROY

what

WALT

fuck

ROY

what

WALT

gotta a little problem here, we

ROY

gosh I

WALT

fucking lemmings

ROY

uhhhhhhhhh — wha?

WALT

you know what they say, what say about, how lemmings,
they get together in the little groups, and run off the sides of cliffs,
committing their little mass suicides

ROY

okay

WALT

making a film about that

ROY

sure why not

WALT

'cuz who wouldn't

ROY

lemmings

WALT

all set up to do a film about

ROY

yes

WALT

how they

ROY

yes

WALT
off cliffs

ROY
see

WALT
but they're not

ROY
they're

WALT
not jumping, not grouping, not killing themselves, not once, filming for weeks

ROY
getting expensive

WALT
not doing what they're supposed to do

ROY
okay

WALT
and if

ROY
why are we under the impression?

WALT
they commit suicide?

ROY
where did we hear that?

WALT
I've heard it

ROY
yeah I

WALT
guy who draws pictures for me

ROY
who

WALT
says he saw

ROY
where

WALT
a picture of this

ROY
> what

WALT
> somewhere at some point, saw some picture of lemmings, some
> drawing somewhere,
> lemmings falling off, but these lemmings, these lemmings, these
> lemmings right here,
> > Walt points to a cliff, points to a bunch of lemmings
> > Close on lemmings, lemmings just hanging out and
> these lemmings don't

ROY
> just sort of

WALT
> sitting there, just don't jump, waiting for them to jump, no jumping,
> then what's this about,
> no one's interested in lemmings unless they're killing themselves,
> don't

ROY
> you

WALT
> can't just

ROY
> if you

WALT
> really up shit's creek here, 'cuz we got these distributors and people,
> they're waiting and expecting and thinking, make me look bad,
> make me look like a real dumbass if

ROY
> you say they do this, jumping

WALT
> yeah

ROY
> you say they do this, then couldn't

WALT
> yeah

ROY
> just to

WALT
> yeah

ROY

save time, save money, save trouble, you could

WALT

. . .

ROY

I dunno

WALT

. . .

ROY

you know record players, if you, you know if you drop something
on a record player, turntable, while the turntable is going real fast,
if you, the thing, it just sorta flings across

WALT

oh that's fun

ROY

across the room, it

WALT

yeah

ROY

if you were to make a bunch of turntables, and film, film from
down the cliff, looking up, looking up at the edge of the cliff,
film that way, help, just *help* the lemmings jump off the cliff

WALT

since they

ROY

can't do it themselves

WALT

so much fun Roy

ROY

if the truth is

WALT

that lemmings like to commit suicide in big groups

ROY

if the truth is, if that's the truth, then it's not untrue to show

WALT

yeah

ROY

to recreate the truth, because

WALT

and then the camera Cuts back to

Interior,
Walt's office,
night.
a good day's
ROY
so nice
WALT
work
ROY
happy you
WALT
have a purpose in life
(WALT *takes out a bottle of vodka.*)
ROY
just thought you thought I was just the money guy
WALT
very good at
ROY
numbers and
WALT
I do the more
ROY
creative
WALT
sure
ROY
but some time's nice to make
WALT
hard work
ROY
nice to think you think I could
WALT
but
ROY
I know
WALT
Cut to

WALT
Scene 2,
Unions.
Exterior. Day.
Parking lot.
People. Standing outside.
With signs.
Looking mad.

Interior. Car.
I'm in the car.
Looking at the people, lots of people,
standing around with signs,
Shit
ROY
lots of
WALT
people
ROY
wanting more money is all
WALT
who
ROY
artists, animators, some writers, people who draw, people who ink
WALT
work for me
ROY
sure
WALT
no, leaving
ROY
striking
WALT
shit
ROY
striking, asking for
WALT
more money

ROY
a union, wanting
WALT
demanding
ROY
wanting to make a little union, a little group, that's all, a little
WALT
so they can have power
ROY
leverage
WALT
thought we were all friends
ROY
okay
WALT
forcing me to
ROY
asking
WALT
this is war
ROY
no
WALT
this is war
ROY
no
WALT
Interior, studios. Day.
Empty
shit
ROY
can be fixed
WALT
People leave and people left
ROY
taking it personally
WALT
what am I supposed to do

ROY

    hard to admit one is wrong

WALT

    did nothing wrong

ROY

    not saying you did

WALT

    work so hard

ROY

    everyone works very hard

WALT

    but me, me more than anyone, I just

ROY

    I know

WALT

    not personally, with my hands, sure I don't,

    not with my hands,

    not personally, I don't make the movies, the pictures,

    the theme parks, the places, the buildings, the world,

    I don't, I can't, I could, only there's a limit,

    one person, can do so much, only so much,

    one person

ROY

    you do so much

WALT

    have so many ideas, one person can only

ROY

    of course, bring in people

WALT

    who

ROY

    workers

WALT

    work for me

ROY

    people working

WALT

    working hard

ROY

of course, and I would say

WALT

(Points to tissue.)

Pass me a hankie will ya

ROY

you feel like they don't trust you,

you don't have their best interests in your interests

WALT

thanks

(Coughs into the handkerchief.)

ROY

in your mind, in

WALT

get tense

ROY

relax and

WALT

carrying the load all by myself

ROY

people

WALT

and everyone leaves

(WALT downs pills and vodka and)

ROY

no

WALT

you'll leave me

ROY

no

WALT

abandon me

ROY

no

WALT

you'll get tired of me

ROY

no

WALT
weary
ROY
no
WALT
weary of Walt
ROY
no
WALT
no, I know I'm difficult, I know
ROY
this problem can be fixed
WALT
Then fix it.
ROY
. . .
WALT
Then fix it.
ROY
. . .
WALT
Then fix it then, if it can be fixed
ROY
means saying you're wrong,
it means saying sort of
to some degree that you're wrong
WALT
no
ROY
it means
WALT
no
ROY
it means giving them some of what they want,
because they work so hard for you
the people working for you,
having families, having kids, prices go up,
and just a little more

WALT

I give so much

ROY

want a little more,

just a little more,

not much

WALT

too much

ROY

not much, just a little

WALT

shit

ROY

don't give them *everything* they want,

no, sure, not,

we give a little

WALT

just yesterday said I wouldn't give

ROY

just means doing something a little different from what you said

you said you'd do

WALT

saying I'm wrong

ROY

it means

WALT

no

ROY

it means

WALT

No no, no no, no no, no.

ROY

. . .

WALT

You say it.

ROY

. . .

WALT
You say you were wrong.

ROY
. . .

WALT
You. You say you were wrong.
You say you were the problem.
You say it was your fault.
You say you were the wrong one,
the one standing in my way,
you say that Walt wanted to give them more money,
but you refused but now you've

ROY
not really what I was

WALT
because I'm Walt and you're Roy and being Walt means something
different than being

ROY
how

WALT
and Walt means

ROY
what

WALT
lots of things

ROY
you mean

WALT
depend on my name

ROY
so

WALT
you disagree? you say your name means what my name means, that
your name is worth what my name is worth, that people need your

ROY
no

WALT
you disagree

ROY

no

WALT

you agree

ROY

I think

WALT

people actually name their children after me, people

ROY

I see

WALT

a sign of affection

ROY

when children name their children after a parent

WALT

No.

That's not,

no

ROY

oh you mean

WALT

other people, not my children, other people name their, article in

Time magazine,

and it listed the most popular names to name your boys and my

name

ROY

number one?

WALT

Three but

ROY

people pay tribute

WALT

yes

ROY

that's nice

WALT

all the time it happens, and someday my daughter will also name

one of her kids after

ROY

okay

WALT

someday,

but that's not,

other people, people I don't know even,

name their kids,

which I think is really

ROY

nice

WALT

If you really care about me,

if you really appreciate everything I've done for you,

haven't I, haven't I?

Haven't I don't so much for you

ROY

yes

WALT

what would you have without me, what would you be doing, what

would you have

ROY

wouldn't have much I guess

WALT

you'd work in a factory or insurance or

ROY

no, yes, sure

WALT

could never be a doctor or

ROY

well

WALT

not the right type of brain, grades weren't

ROY

different type of

WALT

don't you appreciate

ROY

I do and I

WALT

care about me

ROY

I do

WALT

and like me

ROY

sure I

WALT

you're my brother, and I've done so much for

ROY

. . . okay

WALT

you say you're wrong, say it was your fault, take the blame

ROY

. . . okay

WALT

fix it

ROY

okay

WALT

don't ask for much, Roy, don't need

ROY

okay

WALT

but don't I deserve it?

ROY

you really

WALT

Cut to

WALT
Scene 3,
Cities.

Exterior, airplane, in the sky,
an airplane flying, flying from California
Interior, airplane flying,
interior, Walt and Roy, interior airplane, flying.
Flying somewhere.
Flying from California
to Florida.
Flying on business.
Flying on important business.
What business?
None of your business.
Secret business.

And Walt cracks his neck and cracks his back,
and hurts, and takes his pills
takes his pills,
(Pours vodka. Takes the pills.)
takes his pills,
(Drinks.)
and it hurts,
all over it hurts,
Close on Walt hurting,
he's okay
he's okay
Shit. Fuck.
(Smokes.)
He says to Roy,
would be nice to get a back rub here

ROY
can't

WALT
Roy

ROY
really

WALT
you
ROY
miss my home.
Miss my wife.
My kids.
My dog.
WALT
oh
ROY
The dog died. I miss my dog. Back broke.
Wife had to take him in. Put him down.
All by herself. I was away. The kids cried. She cried.
She had to hold his little body when
the doctor injected him with the poison,
had to hold his little, he whimpered, his leg spasm'd, then stopped,
then dead.
I wasn't there. I wasn't there, I was here, I wasn't there.
And they miss me. I think. They miss me.
It's been days weeks months
WALT
years since I saw my family, because there's work
ROY
I think I'm missed, are you missed? you think you're
WALT
   Cut to,
   Walt says to Roy,
time to work
ROY
. . . okay
WALT
'cuz now I'm going to make a city,
an actual, a city
ROY
okay
WALT
because I've made a theme park, and that's like a city
ROY
not really

WALT
thinking about how it's kind of perfect,
thinking about how well it works

ROY
you

WALT
solved the problem of problems

ROY
it's a

WALT
perfect

ROY
nice enough place

WALT
you agree

ROY
I suppose

WALT
what

ROY
one feels safe when one is there

WALT
no accidents, no deaths

ROY
well

WALT
no

ROY
well

WALT
no

ROY
they happen

WALT
death happens, but not

ROY
happens off site, far away, miles away, people are removed if

WALT
Yes

ROY

if they're sick, if they're

WALT

say it like it's cheating.

ROY

not a place where problems don't exist.

The problems there are there, they're just dealt with

behind the scenes, back rooms, underground, far away

WALT

there's no need to bother everyone, there's no need to make a big

deal out of it, show it, see it,

because dealing with problems in a way that makes a big deal, isn't

really helping anyone.

People panic.

People get scared.

People think problems are problems because they see problems as

problems, but if you don't see the problems to see the problems as

problems, there aren't problems.

   Close on Roy.

   Close on Walt.

   Close on Roy and Closer on Roy and Closer and

ROY

Okay.

WALT

It works.

ROY

Okay

WALT

want to make a city like I've made a theme park, an actual city,

a place where people live and sleep and work and eat and

ROY

could be

WALT

best thing I've ever done

ROY

difficult

WALT

with its own government,

government that I've invented

ROY
could be

WALT
place where everyone rents and no one owns property because owning a house means you have to take care of the house and who knows how to take care of a house, I don't, you have experts for this, experts for everything, and everyone does only what they're good at, and no one does what they're not good at, and this means everything works better

ROY
okay but

WALT
and if you live there you don't own property which means

ROY
no voting rights

WALT
no taxes

ROY
no say

WALT
experts will say when experts have something to say, too much

ROY
controlling

WALT
my idea of the perfect place

ROY
people have to

WALT
no. no.

ROY
seems a bit too

WALT
not getting it

ROY
no

WALT
thinking ahead

ROY

you're

WALT

Cut to

if you think of how people have lived for

ROY

decades

WALT

centuries, and it doesn't work, and people aren't much happier, and

we're moving

ROY

kinda like

WALT

into a future

ROY

it's so fast

WALT

we control the atom,

we can take the atom

and see it

and break it

and reassemble

ROY

never thought

WALT

going into space, going to the moon, getting

ROY

faster

WALT

better, older, living older than we've ever lived

ROY

sure

WALT

but

ROY

see

WALT

And close on Walt.

There's a guy in Irvine,
has a place, a lab, a building, the guy freezes bodies,
the guy tells me that he can take a body
and freeze the body, the head, the head of the body,
just the head, because that's where everything is,
everything that matters is in the head, freeze the head,
when the time comes,
and when the time comes,
when we know how to fix everything there is to fix in the body,
everything that can go wrong,
when that time comes,
we can unfreeze the head,
and give the head a better body, a better body that doesn't die

ROY

seems a little

WALT

this will happen, someday, my city, my place, the place I make,
this will be the place where people can go and live forever

   (A cell phone on the table rings. ROY *picks up.)*

ROY

Yeah.
Okay.
Sure.

   *(*ROY *hangs up.)*

So I just talked to the board

WALT

just then

ROY

just, yeah

WALT

you

ROY

talked to the board

WALT

and

ROY

they really like the idea of going to Florida and building a new
park, a new

WALT

no, that's

ROY

not what you wanted

WALT

to make a city

ROY

think it sounds really

WALT

impressive

ROY

costly

WALT

that's

ROY

the sense I got, from

WALT

I think

ROY

they think money's

WALT

awful

ROY

important, just being practical

WALT

how much

ROY

it'll bring in

WALT

it won't, it's a city

ROY

cities

WALT

cost

ROY

too much, but a theme park

WALT

no

ROY
    well that's what they

WALT
    so

ROY
    so

WALT
    so?

ROY
    you don't control the money

WALT
    so

ROY
    so

WALT
    so?

ROY
    the board controls the money, and you don't control the board,
    you like to think you do, but you don't

WALT
    it's

ROY
    your company

WALT
    yes

ROY
    you made it

WALT
    yes

ROY
    but companies, big ones, when they're as big

WALT
    has to be, no other way

ROY
    yes, but that means, you're not the only

WALT
    my decisions

ROY

many people weighing in

WALT

shitty situation

ROY

this is the truth

WALT

something to deal with

ROY

money controls the board, and money controls the people with the
money

WALT

gotta be a way

ROY

make a city make money

WALT

must be a way

ROY

really don't see a way

WALT

You won't see how if you don't want to, you don't want to is all,
you

ROY

not really, I

WALT

just don't want to, if you really wanted to have a good idea for me,
you would have a good idea for me.

ROY

. . . that doesn't seem like a fair thing to say

WALT

. . . just an observation

ROY

ideas take time

WALT

haven't got

ROY

Wait a minute

WALT
what

ROY
wait a minute

WALT
what

ROY
. . . might have an idea

WALT
what.

ROY
Building

WALT
yes

ROY
building buildings

WALT
what about it?

ROY
takes time

WALT
yes

ROY
takes time to build a building

WALT
building's slow

ROY
why

WALT
uh

ROY
not always slow, not slow for cities

WALT
shit

ROY
you see

WALT
maybe

ROY

permits

WALT

approval

ROY

for building

WALT

okay now I'm lost

ROY

waiting for permits takes long, costs money

WALT

yeah yeah yeah

ROY

You go to the government, you say I'd like to build a water fountain,
a little water fountain,
a water fountain 'bout this big,
and you need to fill out a paper, submit the paper

WALT

lawyers look at the paper, say okay or not okay

ROY

send in the paper, wait to get the paper back

WALT

days weeks

ROY

months pass, time passes, money waits, and this little fountain
finally gets built. Times it by hundreds and thousands

WALT

money people, board people

ROY

want another theme park, another bigger, not Disneyland but
Disney World

WALT

and bigger takes time

ROY

so.
here's the deal.
If we tell Florida that we plan to build a city,
promise to build a city,

then they'll make us a district.

And if we're a district,

then we can do things a company can't do.

If we're a district, we can approve our own building permits.

And this saves money.

But the board has to promise that we'll build a city on the property.

That we'll build a place where people live and work and

WALT

oh that's good

ROY

if we're a district we can build anything we want

WALT

and

ROY

getting special tax privileges

WALT

sure

ROY

board will

WALT

like that

ROY

and also

WALT

yeah

ROY

power of eminent domain

WALT

oh that's fun

ROY

'cuz now you're

WALT

Six months later

ROY

now you're

WALT

buying shitloads of land

ROY

okay

WALT

so cheap and

ROY

careful that you

WALT

bet the board's happy with

ROY

liking all the land

WALT

making blueprints

ROY

okay, you know if you

WALT

moving faster than I

ROY

see this bit of land here

WALT

oh yeah I want that

ROY

offered the farmer money

WALT

already have a blueprint for how I want to use

ROY

said he'd say yes

WALT

good because

ROY

except that

WALT

wants more money?

ROY

no, happy with

WALT

what's the hold up

ROY

got a tree on the property

WALT
so
ROY
big old tree
WALT
so
ROY
really big
WALT
and
ROY
will only sell the land if we agree to keep the tree
WALT
why
ROY
just not cut it down
WALT
what kind of
ROY
and he's a real
WALT
controlling
ROY
real nice guy
WALT
already have blueprints for the
ROY
talked to him a lot
WALT
can't have a tree there
ROY
he's a farmer
WALT
fucks with the design
ROY
reminds me of
WALT
what a dickhead

ROY

lot like our dad, you know

WALT

was a dickhead?

ROY

was a farmer

WALT

so

ROY

and it's one request, and I think we can

WALT

you think

ROY

we're

WALT

giving him more money than he's probably ever seen, in his life,
we're

ROY

said to me

WALT

don't care

ROY

says it's important, this tree, seems silly, but that's how it is,
important, 'cuz it's old,
'cuz it's been in the family for a long long time,

WALT

so

ROY

says it was his father's father's, his father's father planted it, planted
it when his wife died

WALT

just a tree

ROY

says it's the most important thing in the world to him, says it has

WALT

can't

ROY

won't

WALT
make one exception

ROY
just

WALT
no

ROY
really?

WALT
I'm planning the perfect city, the perfect place

ROY
and if he doesn't

WALT
tell him we'll exercise our powers

ROY
really?

WALT
we run a district

ROY
it's just a

WALT
and districts have powers, we have

ROY
it's a

WALT
a right to

ROY
you

WALT
don't tell me what I

ROY
can't do that to a

WALT
rather give him a nice sum of money, it's more money than

ROY
just a tree

WALT
exactly

ROY

getting your way

WALT

need the land 'cuz the blueprints

ROY

careless

WALT

there is a limit, there is a limit, a person cannot care about

ROY

no

WALT

important work, moved into the real world now, changing how
the world works, how the world does what it does, how the world
sees, how the world, I mean, you can't change the world and have
a small life at the same time, you can't

ROY

you're

WALT

not operating on that scale, this is, bigger scale, have to be one
of the most important people who ever lived, what's the point
unless you're one of the most important people who ever lived,
what's the point, people are, most people, completely unimportant,
most people, a waste, a

ROY

don't force him out

WALT

you did it, you gave me this power, you

ROY

if you

WALT

no choice now

ROY

then I'll tell the press you forced a poor farmer
a widowed farmer off his land and then,
because of a tree, a stupid

WALT

my right to

ROY
look really, really bad

WALT
. . .

ROY
I will.
I will tell.

WALT
. . .

ROY
. . .

WALT
shit

ROY
. . .

WALT
all I wanted was to make the perfect city.

ROY
. . .

WALT
I'm going to remember this

ROY
in the end

WALT
I'm going to remember

ROY
getting what you want

WALT
no

ROY
mostly

WALT
pass me a hankie, will ya

ROY
really for the best

(WALT *coughs. He coughs up a lot of blood.*)

WALT
. . .

ROY

. . .

WALT

Shit.

ROY

That's a lot of blood.

WALT

Fuck.

ROY

That's a lot of blood.

WALT

. . .

ROY

. . .

WALT

Cut to

WALT
> **Scene 4,**
> **Sick.**

> Interior, Doctor's office.
> Then, outside the office.
> Day. Exterior.
> Sun. Exterior.
> Roy
> Roy
Don't tell.

ROY
> I won't.

WALT
> Don't tell.

ROY
> Okay.

WALT
> No one knows except for you.

ROY
> Is there time?

WALT
> Not much

ROY
> it's

WALT
> the pains

ROY
> okay

WALT
> wasn't calcification, like they

ROY
> oh

WALT
> something else, something eating me from the inside, eating my
> lungs from the inside, cells taking over cells, eating me

ROY
> not much

WALT

time

ROY

tell your wife

WALT

No

ROY

should tell your wife, your kid

WALT

No one knows, board can't know,

board can't know, just bought a lot a land,

they think it's for a park, but it's for more, more than a park,

they gotta go through with it, it's for my city, gotta do the city,

gotta do the city, gonna do this, last thing I do,

gotta do it right, gotta get it done, not much time,

they think I'm going

and going for good, they'll say no, to whatever I say, they'll say no,

they'll know I'm going and going for good, can't go, gonna go,

maybe not

ROY

But your wife

WALT

No one knows, 'cept for you, no, you tell you die, you tell I'll kill you,

you tell you're gone, you better not tell, not you, better,

Cut to

(*WALT puts on some music: Schumann.*)

(*Pours vodka.*)

(*Takes pills.*)

(*Drinks vodka.*)

(*Smokes.*)

(*Looks at bloody handkerchief.*)

(*Gets up.*)

(*Takes the handkerchief over to the trashcan. Puts it in the trash-can.*)

(*Pulls out a wad of handkerchiefs from his back pocket. Looks for a clean handkerchief, but . . .*)

(*. . . one after another, all his handkerchiefs seem to be stained with blood . . .*)

(. . . one after another, he tosses out bloody handkerchiefs . . .)
(. . . finally, he finds a clean handkerchief, blows his nose, and returns to his chair.)
(Takes out another cigarette.)
(Lights it.)
(Smokes.)
(Turns off music.)
(Back to the show.)

WALT
   Scene 5,
   The Son-in-Law.

RON MILLER
   such a fan, I really like

WALT
      Interior, day

RON MILLER
   looked up to and

WALT
      Close on Ron

RON MILLER
   watched all the movies

WALT
      Ron talks

RON MILLER
   the lemmings were good, liked the

WALT
      doesn't stop

RON MILLER
   falling off the

WALT
      what?

RON MILLER
   the cliff

WALT
      could you

RON MILLER
   make more movies about sports 'cuz people really like sports

WALT
      Close on mouth moving

RON MILLER
   wouldn't be one to suggest

WALT
      Close on Ron, Ron, son-in-law, Ron

RON MILLER
   'cuz what do I know

WALT

Close on Ron's teeth

RON MILLER

football

WALT

can tell he doesn't floss

RON MILLER

made me the man I am

WALT

lower life expectancy

RON MILLER

so many things, team work, team spirit

WALT

floss and brush regularly

RON MILLER

discipline, get up every morning, four A.M.

WALT

extend a life by

RON MILLER

running and weights, little swimming

WALT

least five years

RON MILLER

think it makes me strong in mind and spirit

WALT

Walt drinks

RON MILLER

your daughter, best thing that ever

WALT

vodka actually thins blood

RON MILLER

adds another perspective, female perspective

WALT

good for the heart

RON MILLER

unique way of seeing the world

WALT

dumbass

RON MILLER
responsibility

WALT
pass me a hankie

RON MILLER
being a husband, being a father

WALT
    (Coughs.)

RON MILLER
see life differently

WALT
when

RON MILLER
feel so needed

WALT
by what?

RON MILLER
by her

WALT
your wife?

RON MILLER
your daughter.

WALT
and then?

RON MILLER
not for me, for them

WALT
you say

RON MILLER
if I'm hurt, out of work, if I die

WALT
shitty line of work

RON MILLER
what, football?

WALT
shitty line of work

RON MILLER
all the things that could happen

WALT

playing football

RON MILLER

friend's skull got crushed, now in a hospital, feeding tubes, machine to breathe, can't remember who he is, forgot his father, forgot his mother, forgot his sister, forgot his dog, dog remembers, remembers by smell, but he, the guy, the guy with the broken skull and broken brain, forgot everything, eyes wide open, but like he's not there, just drool and spit, and can't control how he swallows and so his mouth fills up and it's like he's drowning in his own mouth and so he needs someone there to pour the drool and the spit out of his mouth, and all the money, costs them money, sister took a job to keep him alive, and he's probably in his head thinking if he's thinking, probably thinking "please kill me because I can't stand being such a burden to you," thinking, "you're my sister and you shouldn't be sitting next to me day and night and night day draining my mouth of mouth water," and even though

WALT

life is hard

RON MILLER

couldn't do that, wouldn't do that, get hurt or maybe die, leave the wife and kids or worse wind up like that and be a burden to

WALT

think you're a real

RON MILLER

hero?

WALT

wouldn't say

RON MILLER

would never think

WALT

hardly think

RON MILLER

the kids and two already

WALT

no control

RON MILLER

another on the way

WALT
a kid?

RON MILLER
on the way

WALT
news to me, you have

RON MILLER
responsibility, so I quit, left for good

WALT
would never call that responsible

RON MILLER
football

WALT
shitty

RON MILLER
dangerous sport

WALT
you quit your job

RON MILLER
yes

WALT
and now you don't make money, because

RON MILLER
money's good, but if something ever happened

WALT
big trouble in family town

RON MILLER
taking responsibility

WALT
want from me

RON MILLER
new career I was sort of thinking

WALT
spit it out

DAUGHTER
Dad

WALT
Pan to daughter, she says

DAUGHTER
    Dad

WALT
    Close on Daughter, Walt's Daughter,
    Walt's Daughter all grown up,
    Daddy's little girl, good little girl,
    such a smart little girl, a tough little girl,
    and Walt, he's the apple of her eye,
    he's her hero, her

DAUGHTER
    Dad

WALT
    and Walt says,
  yeah
    and Daughter says

DAUGHTER
    Ron really just

WALT
    what

DAUGHTER
    wants to take better care of

WALT
    who

DAUGHTER
    me

WALT
    you

DAUGHTER
    let's be honest

WALT
    okay

DAUGHTER
    you don't like him

WALT
    who

DAUGHTER
    Ron, you don't

WALT
    he's

DAUGHTER

not much like you, except sometimes, but mostly,

he thinks differently,

and I know you don't like men who play sports,

and I know you don't like men who are bigger than you,

and I know you don't,

you're just a little intimidated by him, that's all,

but you should get over that,

because he's really good to me, and I know you want me to be with

someone who's good to me,

right?

WALT

but he's

DAUGHTER

don't I deserve

WALT

trying to sneak in, trying to get in, trying to take over

RON MILLER

no, I really

WALT

wants to be my successor, take over the business

RON MILLER

just wanted a job, I'd sweep floors if you let me

WALT

take over, Roy takes over, if anything happens to me, Roy takes over

DAUGHTER

dad

WALT

you need to

DAUGHTER

maybe just an apprentice of some kind

WALT

no experience

RON MILLER

teach me how you do what you do

WALT

no way to

RON MILLER

better position to take care of

WALT

you don't, I will

RON MILLER

want to

WALT

making it my responsibility

RON MILLER

trying to make a new

WALT

because

DAUGHTER

another boy on the way

WALT

boy

RON MILLER

two kids already

WALT

gonna name the boy?

DAUGHTER

dunno

WALT

how

DAUGHTER

I don't

WALT

of course you

RON MILLER

give me the opportunity to

WALT

How come you never named any of your kids after me?
I mean, what's up with that?

DAUGHTER

I dunno

WALT

just wondering why

DAUGHTER

not what really we're talking about

WALT

seems odd, seems strange

DAUGHTER
doesn't really matter

WALT
if it doesn't matter

RON MILLER
teach me what you know

WALT
gonna be a boy

RON MILLER
follow in your footsteps

WALT
sign of respect

DAUGHTER
needs a job

RON MILLER
think we have a lot in common

WALT
if you really

RON MILLER
I love animals

WALT
doesn't make me feel better to hear that you like me, makes me
feel worse to think that someone like you likes me. Okay?

RON MILLER
sorry. Just tell me what you like and I'll do it

WALT
name your kid after me

DAUGHTER
no

WALT
you have two boys and not one is named after

DAUGHTER
no

WALT
seems

DAUGHTER
not important

WALT

then tell me what you are naming the kid,

if not me, then

DAUGHTER

we don't have a name

WALT

bullshit

DAUGHTER

haven't thought about it

WALT

bullshit. Ron, tell me the name

RON MILLER

uh

DAUGHTER

There's no name

WALT

didn't ask you, asked Ron.

Ron, answer the question.

RON MILLER

Thinking maybe Roy?

WALT

Roy.

RON MILLER

After your brother

ROY

had nothing to do with this

DAUGHTER

no right

ROY

please don't put me in the middle of this

WALT

why him and not

DAUGHTER

he's just done so much for us

ROY

please don't put me in the middle

WALT

If you don't name this kid Walt

DAUGHTER
threatening me
WALT
wouldn't call it
DAUGHTER
a threat
WALT
you get nothing.
None of my money.
None of what I own.
You get nothing.
Other family will get everything.
You'll be left out.
Do you want to be left out?
Husband, unemployed.
Has no skills.
Can't do shit.
Shit for brains.
Just muscle. Can throw a ball.
So what. So what.
What good is that.
Not so good.
DAUGHTER
. . .
WALT
. . .
DAUGHTER
just don't think it's a good idea to name my kid the name you're
named
WALT
why?
DAUGHTER
. . .
WALT
why?
DAUGHTER
. . .

WALT

answer the

DAUGHTER

because when I say your name, I think all sorts of things I don't want to think. When I say your name, I think of you, and when I think of you I get all angry, and when I think of you and the way you act, and the way you yell, and the way you threw a tantrum at my wedding and threw cake at people, and I think of the way you yell, and the way you fire people and the way you force people to do what you want them to do, and I know about what you did to Roy

ROY

oh please don't

DAUGHTER

how when you won the Oscar for your film about lemmings

ROY

didn't hurt that much

DAUGHTER

you walked into his office and threw the trophy at his head

ROY

mostly missed my head

DAUGHTER

put a hole in the wall

ROY

didn't hurt too bad

DAUGHTER

when I think these thoughts when I think of the thoughts, I think these thoughts when I say your name, and I get angry, and I get sad, and I get scared, and I know that if I name my kid your name, then anytime I say his name, I'll feel the ways I feel when I think of you, and the kid will see that and the kid will feel that, and the kid will feel like I feel those ways towards him, and he'll feel bad and sad and maybe scared, and over time he'll think I feel about him the way I feel about you, and when he grows up, he'll be really fucked up, and when he grows up, he'll feel like I like his brothers better than him, and because naming him the name you're

WALT

Cut to

music.

Just Walt and Roy.
Bar,
somewhere, somewhere high, in the air,
high up, looking down at
earth, seeing earth spinning around down below
interior, high-in-the-sky bar, night,
vodka, pours some
(Does so.)
(Music: Schumann.)

WALT

Scene 6,
Fans.

FDR saw my movies,
King George was a fan,

Douglas Fairbanks says nice things about me.
Jerry Lewis. Groucho Marx. Fans.
The head of the CIA.
The head of the FBI.
Fans.
Senator McCarthy,
friend and fan.

ROY

. . .

WALT

Wernher von Braun is a good friend
and the same method I use to operate the audioamina, audiaminina,
anima—
the robot presidents at the Hall of Presidents
is the same thing Wernher uses to synchronize rocket launches.
Says he got it from me. 'Cuz

ROY

. . .

WALT

Alan Turing's favorite movie was Snow White,
and when he killed himself, he killed himself by eating a cyanide
coated apple
because he liked the movie so much.

ROY

. . .

WALT

Eisenstein was a fan.
Einstein was a fan.
Mussolini took his kids to see my movies. All of them. Big fans.
Doris Day liked Donald Duck, her favorite character of any character
anywhere, she said.

ROY

. . .

WALT

. . .

ROY

. . .

WALT

silent treatment

ROY

. . .

WALT

Hitler

ROY

. . .

WALT

Hitler said Mickey was silly.

Said mice were dirty.

Said Mickey was a pile of shit.

Really. And look what happened to him

ROY

. . .

WALT

serves him right

ROY

careful

WALT

Cut music

ROY

Walt

WALT

why

ROY

paper printed that comment

WALT

so

ROY

comment about

WALT
Hitler?

ROY
had to have a whole team of

WALT
wasn't like I said anything nice about

ROY
people had to apologize for you

WALT
don't understand what

ROY
things you say

WALT
matters 'cuz I

ROY
Hitler, Mussolini

WALT
also mentioned FDR

ROY
doesn't

WALT
and he's a cripple

ROY
missing the

WALT
point

ROY
and

WALT
shit

ROY
Someone talked and

WALT
just fix it

ROY
on the lemmings movie, someone told and

WALT
small problems

ROY
know it was faked

WALT
easier to

ROY
news people asked an animal expert and the expert said that lemmings don't do that

WALT
what

ROY
jump off cliffs, they don't, never did, not true

WALT
I heard

ROY
you saw

WALT
a picture

ROY
drawn by

WALT
guy I know

ROY
from a comic book

WALT
yeah I saw a picture of lemmings jumping off a

ROY
said what we did was animal cruelty

WALT
bullshit

ROY
news people claiming animal cruelty, because of the turntables

WALT
claiming that I

ROY
no

WALT
who

ROY

claiming my son, my son was responsible, claiming, because his
name, and because he was the producer but

WALT

not my

ROY

wasn't his idea, he didn't

WALT

he produced it

ROY

just a kid and

WALT

think I'm a jerk?

ROY

really hurt my family

WALT

wanna punch me? punch me, go ahead and punch, go ahead

ROY

the whole ordeal hurt my son, hurt my wife,
wife feels like I

WALT

small problems

ROY

hurt the family

WALT

your wife

ROY

said she doesn't love me anymore.
Wife said she fell out of love and can't get it back.
Said she tried. Said we tried.
Said it's just not there.
Said she won't leave me.
Said she doesn't want to leave me,
just doesn't love me but she'll stay,
she'll stay, and I guess we'll

WALT

. . .

ROY

. . .

WALT

. . . sorry I threw my Oscar at your head

ROY

just

WALT

Interior. Work. My office. My studios

ROY

You shouldn't come back around they're starting to

WALT

Shouldn't where

ROY

Work. The place. The company. The board

WALT

whose right to

ROY

They shouldn't see you, looking sick,

really starting to show

WALT

not sure I really

ROY

starting

WALT

to notice

ROY

to talk

WALT

not looking too bad

ROY

wondering about you

WALT

thought I was getting better

ROY

worse actually

WALT

look at myself in the mirror

ROY
every day?
WALT
sure I do
ROY
and that's why, looking every day, harder to see the decline,
but when you step back,
when you're not you,
when you see what others see, you can see, you don't
WALT
getting better
ROY
getting
WALT
Cut to
ROY
but things are moving along
WALT
what does that mean?
ROY
takes time
WALT
no time
ROY
patience
WALT
said nothing
ROY
wrong time, wrong place
WALT
the whole thing, the whole project, the city, the
ROY
plans are
WALT
getting trampled
ROY
read between the lines

WALT

load of shit

ROY

being diplomatic

WALT

try too hard to make everyone happy and no one gets happy

ROY

people need to feel they're being heard when

WALT

whose side are you on

ROY

not about

WALT

sides

ROY

there's

WALT

always a side

ROY

doing what's right

WALT

is a side

ROY

no one will be happy all the time

WALT

small minded

ROY

working hard to

WALT

cowfucker

ROY

not sure what that means.

WALT

I get the minutes of the board meetings, I read the minutes of the board meetings

   Close on minutes of the

These are the minutes. I have the minutes of the board meetings, didn't think, did you, didn't think that I get the minutes of the board

meetings, but I have the minutes of the board meetings, and I read
the minutes of the board meetings, and I can't find any talk about

ROY

timing is

WALT

mention of

ROY

pick your battles

WALT

carefully

ROY

yes

WALT

too careful

ROY

bring it up now and

WALT

job is to make sure the city

ROY

in talks about

WALT

gets mentioned on this page

ROY

concerns about

WALT

here the guy says we can't do it, too much money, just focus on the
theme park, ignore the plans

ROY

up for discussion

WALT

told me that if we agreed to make another theme park they'd let me
have my city, that was the deal

ROY

up for discussion

WALT

even promised the state of Florida

ROY

up for discussion

WALT
and you saying nothing, making no objection, not fighting
ROY
is
WALT
agreeing
ROY
how
WALT
nothing comes of
ROY
taking
WALT
nothing
ROY
action is
WALT
flip through the pages, page after page, no response from you
ROY
making it an argument now would
WALT
have all the power
ROY
sorry you
WALT
like you have the atomic bomb, right there, in your hands, could
end it all, could fix it all, could end the war
ROY
war, what war, not a war
WALT
yes
ROY
fighting only
WALT
all the power and you won't use it
ROY
when the time comes

WALT

probably why

ROY

do what I can to

WALT

you're so spineless, such a wimp, won't stand up

ROY

I'm careful

WALT

that's probably why your wife doesn't love you anymore

ROY

. . . .

WALT

Cut to

WALT
>Scene 7,
>The Liberty Tree.

RON MILLER
>had a dream in which this happened,
>same exact,
>this room,
>this place,
>this time,
>and in this dream
>you called me up,
>and said hey let's go get some coffee and a bagel
>and let's have a sit down,
>let's have a bike ride,
>let's play catch,
>let's watch a game,
>let's go grill a steak,
>and drink a beer,
>and get some ice cream

WALT
>Cut to

RON MILLER
>and in this dream when I saw you, you gave me a hug
>and said hey son
>and I said hey Dad,
>and I was so happy because my dad is Walt Disney

WALT
>Cut to

RON MILLER
>my dad is dead, is your dad dead?

WALT
>Cut to

RON MILLER
>moms are

WALT
>Cut to

RON MILLER
dads are

WALT
Cut to
someday I'll be dead, maybe not tomorrow, but

RON MILLER
no

WALT
will happen

RON MILLER
can't

WALT
why

RON MILLER
'cuz you're

WALT
what

RON MILLER
isn't it true

WALT
that people

RON MILLER
living longer

WALT
Cut to
and someday people won't die, not now, making progress, once

RON MILLER
I know this story

WALT
like companies

RON MILLER
you said

WALT
corporations

RON MILLER
you said

WALT
never meant to

RON MILLER
last forever

WALT
a corporation

RON MILLER
you said

WALT
by definition, by definition, by law, a corporation is made to

RON MILLER
end

WALT
die

RON MILLER
gosh that's sad

WALT
when a business' business is done the business is done, that's what a corporation is, but

RON MILLER
I know where this

WALT
but why? why does that have to be the way it has to

RON MILLER
no fair

WALT
no fair

RON MILLER
yeah

WALT
going into a time when everything that was meant to die, doesn't

RON MILLER
if you

WALT
make sure the business is never done

RON MILLER.
make sure

WALT
keeps living

RON MILLER
  heaven

WALT
  changing, evolving

RON MILLER
  never

WALT
    Exterior Disney World, day.
    Disney World, under construction, still being built,
    Exterior Frontier Land,
    Frontier Land where there's a tree,
    big tree

RON MILLER
  Old tree

WALT
  ancient

RON MILLER
  in the middle of

WALT
  frontier land, America land, Hall of Presidents gonna be there, and

RON MILLER
  I love robots

WALT
  decided well we got this tree here, we call it the Liberty Tree, 'cuz it
  represents, uh, Liberty, and good virtues, and America, and patriotism

RON MILLER
  okay

WALT
  America has always been about liberty and letting people do what
  they want

RON MILLER
  wasn't

WALT
  but got this land here with this tree in the way of where stuff was
  supposed to be, in the way of what I wanted, came down here one
  night, had a conversation with the fucking tree, said to him

RON MILLER
  the tree

WALT

getting in the way, of my Liberty, what I want, not free to do, not
like America,

not right to change the plan,

plans and,

change in plans, change in blueprint, used to be there,

over there, right over there, used to be, couldn't be, why couldn't it be?

uhhhhhhhhhh,

tunnel running underground,

would've fucked with the plumbing, the wiring, the electrics,

but couldn't get rid of the tree, had to keep the tree, because of
some deal,

had to, so we *moved* the tree, we drilled holes into the wood,

put in cables,

used a crane,

lifted it out of the ground,

moved it over,

filled the holes with wood plugs,

wood plugs, though,

woods plugs got infected, got a wood disease,

started rotting,

and the disease spread and the whole tree, started rotting,

know what we did?

what we did was we did, we went inside and cleaned out the tree,

and filled its insides with cement,

but then the leaves started to fall off,

so we went through and replaced every leaf,

it's all vinyl,

vinyl leaves,

but still

RON MILLER

. . .

WALT

Close on Liberty Tree.

Close on Ron.

Close on Walt, and Walt says,

there's a lesson here, do you know what the lesson is, I'm teaching
you, I'm teaching you here, what's the lesson, you

RON MILLER

. . .

WALT

. . .

RON MILLER

. . .

WALT

. . .

RON MILLER

nothing wrong with being a bully

WALT

that's right

RON MILLER

like in football

WALT

you know

RON MILLER

how to push through

WALT

touchdowns and goals and shit

RON MILLER

tackling

WALT

okay then

RON MILLER

faces might get broken, cuts and bruises,
mild concussion

WALT

no matter what

RON MILLER

win

WALT

it's for

RON MILLER

the team, not the one

WALT

not the minority, the minority hurts the whole, the thing must
appeal to many

RON MILLER
or else

WALT
what's the point

RON MILLER
I

WALT
will have problems with the board

RON MILLER
they'll

WALT
resist, but you should

RON MILLER
tackle

WALT
yes

RON MILLER
don't

WALT
I'm putting you in

RON MILLER
okay

WALT
you'll fight

RON MILLER
yeah

WALT
for what I want

RON MILLER
you

WALT
want to make sure they don't just turn my city into another theme
park

RON MILLER
okay

WALT
but they'll side with Roy, them and Roy, in real tight, they like Roy,
they won't like you, not at first, but

RON MILLER
I could

WALT
you could

RON MILLER
I could

WALT
turn them against Roy, make Roy

RON MILLER
how?

WALT
spread the word that the whole lemmings scandal was Roy's idea,
get those animal cruelty people on his case,
and remind them that he stood in the way of the animators efforts to unionize,
and if people complain about the labor violations in Florida,
because you can bet there'll be some labor violations in Florida, I mean, how can't there be,
just let them know that was Roy,
and when people get upset about the copyrights

RON MILLER
turning

WALT
free stuff into stuff you have to pay for

RON MILLER
people don't like

WALT
tell them it was

RON MILLER
Roy's idea

WALT
all the lawsuits

RON MILLER
Roy

WALT
removing farmers from their land, forcing them to sell land at a lower price

RON MILLER
  Roy
WALT
  he said it all, not me, he did, it's true, he said, his ideas, not
RON MILLER
  I see
WALT
    cut to
RON MILLER
  Dad?
WALT
  Yes?
RON MILLER
  Where are you going?
WALT
    cut to
RON MILLER
  thank you
WALT
    cut to
RON MILLER
  thank you
WALT
    cut to
  want that kid
RON MILLER
  the kid?
WALT
  the kid that's coming, the name
RON MILLER
  yes
WALT
  wife won't like it
RON MILLER
  it's okay
WALT
  tell her now, she'll

RON MILLER
  yeah

WALT
  wait until

RON MILLER
  later

WALT
  needs to know there are some things

RON MILLER
  name the kid Walt.

WALT
  or Walter

RON MILLER
  either way

WALT
  Walt Junior sounds good

RON MILLER
  promise

WALT
    Cut to
    (Dials a number on his phone as he talks . . .)

WALT
  Scene 8,
  Walt's Wife.

  Hello?
  Hello Wife.
  Hi.
  Yeah.
  It's me.
  Walt.
  Whadareya doin?
  Oh. Okay.
  No, just
  calling
  Just
  Wanted to
  Yes
  Wondered where
  Oh I see
     cut to
  doing fine
     cut to
  thinking about
     cut to
  you know what I like.
  I like, about you I like how
     cut to
  just remembering how we met
     cut to
  drawing, you drawing, you drawing for me,
  working for me, liked how you drew the things I thought up,
  liked how
     cut to
  and I liked that when I first met you, you were working for me
  because if you married me that must've meant that
  you really liked working for me
     cut to

and boy you could really draw
   cut to
draw the things I thought
   cut to
tried some drawing myself the other day, I,
not in such a long time,
   cut to
drew some Mickey Mouses
   cut to
   (Shows drawings.)
think they turned out pretty good, not amazing,
but
   cut to
think I still got it
   cut to
yeah, I'll send them to you, I think they're pretty good, pretty
uhhhhhhhhh
   cut to
Hey so I wanted to
Yeah
Wanted to tell you about
This
   cut to
Just wondering if
   cut to
Thinking about
Future
Thinking
Heard of
   cut to
There's this Guy in Irvine
   cut to
He freezes the bodies
He freezes, well, just the head and
No, it's not gross, it's beautiful,
it's beautiful, it's
   cut to

Not that I'm dying anytime soon
   cut to
Not that I'm dying anytime
   cut to
Not that
   cut to
No, just
   cut to
the future
and wondered
   cut to
would you be interested in that, I could sign you up for,
so you and me,
we get frozen,
and when it's time, if it's time, when it's time,
when the world is safer,
technology better,
we get unfrozen,
and we come back,
and we come back, and
   cut to
and they can rebuild our bodies and
   cut to
and maybe even, if there's anything we wanted changed,
bodies or minds or
anything we wanted removed,
like a bad memory,
or
   cut to
can change anything we want
   cut to
you know, just like a
   cut to
movie
   cut to
and then we come back, better than ever
   cut to

keep on living, together, in the future,
you and
 cut to
you and me in the
 cut to
living
 cut to
okay,
well,
you know just think about it
 cut to
okay, no that's fine
 cut to
no don't worry about—it's
 cut to
daughter's gonna name her next kid after me
 cut to
okay
 cut to
bye
 cut to
 (Coughs. Bad cough.)
 (Takes out a handkerchief, and as he pulls out the handkerchief,
 out comes a pile of very bloody handkerchiefs.)

WALT
> Scene 9,
> God.
>
> *(Clears all of the handkerchiefs from the table in one big swipe of his hand.)*
> Interior. Hospital.
> Night.
> Interior Hospital, what Hospital?
> Secret Hospital,
> no-one-knows-where-I-am secret Hospital.
> And Walt,
> close on Walt.
> In a bed.
> Hard to move with
> Walt hooked up to
> machines.
> shit.
>
> Cut to.
>
> Daughter.
> Enters.
> Asks

DAUGHTER
> are you comfortable?

WALT
> wiggles his toes

DAUGHTER
> cold

WALT.
> wiggles his

DAUGHTER
> blanket

WALT
> cut to

DAUGHTER
> You disappeared, and

WALT
How

DAUGHTER
did I

WALT
know

DAUGHTER
you were here?

WALT
  nods yes

DAUGHTER
This.

WALT
  close on
  (DAUGHTER *takes out bloody handkerchief.*)

DAUGHTER
found a long trail of these

WALT
leading

DAUGHTER
from there to here.

WALT
oh . . .
  (WALT *looks back at the trash can.*)
  cut to
Please don't tell

DAUGHTER
who

WALT
anyone about

DAUGHTER
you

WALT
  cut to

DAUGHTER
Why can't

WALT
you tell

DAUGHTER
anyone?

WALT
important 'cuz

DAUGHTER
you'll

WALT
lose

DAUGHTER
what

WALT
control

DAUGHTER
of your

WALT
city.
   cut to

DAUGHTER
But

WALT
. . .

DAUGHTER
I sorta

WALT
what

DAUGHTER
did

WALT
tell?

DAUGHTER
yes.

WALT
. . . who?
   cut to

DAUGHTER
Mom

WALT
   cut to

DAUGHTER
Ron

WALT
cut to

DAUGHTER
and Ron

WALT
he

DAUGHTER
I think

WALT
he

DAUGHTER
told the board.

WALT
cut to

DAUGHTER
. . .

WALT
shit

DAUGHTER
. . .

WALT
cut to

DAUGHTER
. . .

WALT
fuck

DAUGHTER
I

WALT
cut to

DAUGHTER
really

WALT
don't.
cut to

DAUGHTER
. . .

WALT

. . .

DAUGHTER

. . .

WALT

cut to

DAUGHTER

. . . Ron

WALT

. . .

DAUGHTER

likes his job

WALT

cut to

DAUGHTER

talks all day about

WALT

cut to

DAUGHTER

nice of you to

WALT

cut to

DAUGHTER

talks constantly about

WALT

cut to

DAUGHTER

really thinks you're

WALT

cut to

DAUGHTER

. . .

WALT

cut to

DAUGHTER

Ron doesn't

WALT

cut to

DAUGHTER
anymore, he

WALT
cut to

DAUGHTER
starting to

WALT
he's

DAUGHTER
different

WALT
cut to

DAUGHTER
not the man I

WALT
cut to

DAUGHTER
Walked home in the rain last night

WALT
cut to

DAUGHTER
thinking about

WALT
cut to

DAUGHTER
Do you ever miss your mother

WALT
cut to

DAUGHTER
do you want a pillow

WALT
cut to

DAUGHTER
do you want some water

WALT
cut to

DAUGHTER
Thinking about other places

WALT
   cut to
DAUGHTER
  wish I had a
WALT
   cut to
DAUGHTER
  touch your face one last
WALT
   cut to
DAUGHTER
  . . . think it's time I
WALT
  stay
DAUGHTER
  and
WALT
  lonely
DAUGHTER
  yeah
WALT
   cut to
DAUGHTER
  . . .
WALT
   cut to
DAUGHTER
  so much
WALT
   cut to
DAUGHTER
  Sorry, I told people that you're dying, I just thought
WALT
   cut to
DAUGHTER
  can't change
WALT
  everyone

DAUGHTER
> how I feel

WALT
> course I can

DAUGHTER
> you

WALT
> can be sick

DAUGHTER
> doesn't mean I

WALT
>> cut to

DAUGHTER
> . . .

WALT
>> cut to

DAUGHTER
> You

WALT
> sure

DAUGHTER
> don't live well with people

WALT
>> cut to

DAUGHTER
> more like a god than a person

WALT
> nicest thing anyone's ever

DAUGHTER
> not sure that's a good thing

WALT
> thank you
>> he wiggles his toes,
> thank you,
>> he wiggles,
>> cut to

WALT
  Scene 10,
  Cryonics.

   (Music: the lullaby.)
   Exterior. World. Day.
   Interior. Place.
   Night.
   Interior. Building.
   Building in Irvine.
   No windows.
   Interior. Building. Cold.
   Very cold. Steel.
   Stainless.
   Interior. Building where men wear white lab coats.
   Interior. Day, building, men,
   lab coats,
   me, blue gown,
   very cold,
   interior . . .

   Me.
   Roy.
   and
ROY
  so
WALT
   close on Walt, close on Walt,
   and close on Walt, and Walt says to Roy
  I'm about to go
   Walt says to Roy,
   and thinks this will make Roy sad

   and freeze on Roy and

   Walt thinks, Roy's so cold, that Roy, so cold, ice, I call him ice,
   just no reaction, he says
ROY
  okay

WALT

just says

ROY

okay

WALT

and freeze on Walt and close on Walt.

And Walt thinks, well I'll tell Mr. Ice something, something to really

ROY

okay

WALT

get a reaction out of him, and Walt says,

I gave Ron your job

ROY

okay

WALT

gave Ron your job, how you were supposed to take over for me,

well I just gave it all to

ROY

okay

WALT

and freeze on Roy and freeze on, close on,

we can tell from the close up that he's really pissed off about

ROY

okay

WALT

really pissed off, serves him right, pissed off,

you can tell, can't you tell? you can tell, oh sure yeah you,

and

ROY

whatever you want, I just

WALT

close on his eyes, his tears, cut to

ROY

not really that upset

WALT

he is, and he says

ROY

Ron's not so

WALT
he thinks Ron's not so,
not so what?

ROY
smart

WALT
strong, he's

ROY
being

WALT
a bully

ROY
yep

WALT
like he should
I think

ROY
he'll hurt

WALT
the company

ROY
yes

WALT
so dumb

ROY
he'll

WALT
drive the company into the ground

ROY
yes

WALT
I know

ROY
you know

WALT
I know

ROY
you

WALT
    want the whole thing

ROY
    the company

WALT
    when I'm gone

ROY
    to fail

WALT
    yes

ROY
    because

WALT
    I want

ROY
    see how

WALT
    much they need me.
        Cut to
        Walt, on a table.
        Cut to Roy.
        Cut to Roy

ROY
    feeling

WALT
    remorse

ROY
    better

WALT
    oh he's sorry

ROY
    things with the wife

WALT
    worse

ROY
    better

WALT
    cut to

ROY
she likes me again
WALT
cut to
ROY
touches me again
WALT
Close on Walt
ROY
think we love each other again
WALT
Walt on a table, in the lab in
ROY
When the board found out you were dying
WALT
ready to
ROY
we sat down and had a talk about your city
WALT
stop the body
ROY
best if we turn it into another theme park
WALT
and drain the fluids, cut to
ROY
hold onto the
WALT
machines attached
ROY
more conservative
WALT
close on tubes
ROY
just
WALT
and heart stops
ROY
makes more sense

WALT
Walt's
ROY
financially
WALT
cut to
ROY
in the spirit
WALT
close on neck
ROY
what you wanted
WALT
close on saw
ROY
dedicated to
WALT
cut to
ROY
you
WALT
close on saw cutting into
ROY
and technology
WALT
cut through Walt's neck
ROY
and the world, pavilions devoted to the all the countries of the
WALT
and cut through spine, hard to cut through,
cut the spine, spine snaps.

The spine,
and Walt,
close on Walt,
close on Walt's head
severed head,
close on

freeze
freeze the
freeze the head, Walt's head,
Walt is just a head,
close on Walt's head in freeze.
frozen

cut to

Roy. And Roy cries.
(ROY *doesn't cry.*)

Roy cries, everyone cries,
wife cries,
daughter,
Ron
and even a dog, there's a dog there,
and even the dog cries,
everyone cries

and then they stop,
and they do nothing,
because now that I'm gone,
no one does anything,
now that I'm gone the world just stops, right?
right? that's
the world has stopped is waiting for me to return,
waiting for me to defrost and show them the way . . .

And Walt
in the end
Walt sees
everything
in his head, where everything is
in this head, sees everything that's in his head

because
what death is,
what death is, is real slow, it's a slow fade, a slow
and eternal fade, two seconds in real time,
but an eternity in mind time,

and that is what heaven is,
what heaven is, is whatever is
in Walt's head when Walt's head's dead,
when Walt's brain shuts down,
and the brain it's seeing itself,
and it's seeing itself slow down,
and it's seeing itself see itself real slow,
and time stretches,
so it's like that, it's a real slow fade out,
and as the brain shuts down,
the brain thinks about itself,
thinks about thinking about itself,
inside itself,
flashbacks and flashes forward,
and freeze on
everything it contains,
and it contains,
what I think I think is a real good life, heaven,
a real
and Walt is happy
and Walt is loved
and Walt is happier than he's been
better than he's ever been
smarter than he's been
and everyone misses him,
and it's a real
slow,
a real
slow
fade . . .

(Long pause. WALT *looks as if he's about to say "out" . . .)*
(Lullaby suddenly stops playing.)

End of Play